FIELD GUIDE

Retriever Drills

Training Your Retriever At Home, In The Field, And On The Water

Benjamin H. Schleider III
& Anthony Z. Roettger

Field Guide to™ Series

Wilderness
Adventures
Press, Inc.™

Belgrade, Montana

Field Guide to™ Series

Published by Wilderness Adventures Press, Inc.™
45 Buckskin Road
Belgrade, MT 59714
866-400-2012
Website: www.wildadvpress.com
email: books@wildadvpress.com

First Edition 2008

Printed in the United States of America

ISBN 978-1932098-55-6 (1-932098-55-0)

Table of Contents

Legend

Dog

Handler

Dummy

Tree

Food Dish

Bird Dummy

Scented Dummy

On Lead/Checkcord

Direction for Dog

Direction for Handler

Dog Roaming Free

Path of Thrown Object

Hedge/Ditch

Sidewalk/Driveway

Introduction

The Field Guide to Retriever Drills is a companion to our "Urban Gun Dogs: Training Flushing Dogs For Home and Field".

This handy pocket guide can be taken into the field while conducting your dog training drills. A number of these drills can be done indoors or in your back yard, as well as in the field. We have divided the guide into both indoor and outdoor drills. We have 19 indoor drills and 38 outdoor field and water drills ranging from basic drills to advanced drills.

It is an enjoyable way to spend time with your dog while improving his or her retrieving ability. You will find this pocket drill guide to be an invaluable training tool; one that you will always have with you in your training vest or bag.

Chip Schleider & Tony Roettger

How to Use This Book

In using this drill guide, we suggest that you first carefully review your training plan and each drill you wish to concentrate on for a particular session. We cannot overemphasize the importance of reviewing the drill guide before you and your dog hit the training area. In addition, it is important to understand that we are primarily spaniel trainers. Spaniels for essentially historical reasons are trained to sit at the word "hup." Please substitute the word "sit" for "hup" if your predilections take you in that direction. In addition, we use the following whistle commands: one "pip" on the whistle to "hup" or sit; two "pips" to turn your dog while quartering, and four "pips" to recall your dog.

For maximum success, we suggest that you master one drill prior to moving to the next phase. We have constructed our guide with both indoor and outdoor sections. You will have to judge whether or not you wish to start your dog indoors. If you elect to start outdoors, remember outdoor training contains many more distractions than training inside. Be patient and expect your dog to take longer if you start outside.

The key to good results is to evaluate the amount of time you have to dedicate to your canine friend as well as assess your objectives in gun dog training. Plan to dedicate at least thirty minutes daily to training—do not plan for two days of two-hour sessions during the weekend with no training during the week. Consistent, frequent, and relatively short periods of training will enable your dog to make significant strides. Plan also to incorporate little five-minute training sessions such as having your dog sit for increasingly longer periods of time, or place training during your normal home routine.

Remember, training is best done in moderation. Many small lessons spanning minutes are better than one single two-hour block. Training in moderation means that both you and the dog are fresh for each session, and quit on a positive note. Dogs have a relatively short attention span, and will lose interest over time. Plan your lessons to be short with rest between them. If you tend to have a short fuse, a short lesson will help you with patience as well. Also, there is no timeline for achieving a specific level of performance. When the dog has fully mastered a lesson, move to the next level.

One final note. We have found that locating suitable training space is often the major challenge to training a gun dog. For example, if you must train exclusively in urban areas you face fundamentally different challenges in training your dog than if you have ready access to rural training facilities. If you clearly identify your training area limitations, you can put in place a plan to overcome them. Again, do not hesitate to adjust your training and drills to reflect your training environment.

About the Authors

Chip Schleider is an avid amateur spaniel trainer and upland game hunter. Chip is the co-author with Tony Roettger of Urban Gun Dogs: Training Flushing Dogs for Home and Field. Chip also writes short stories; one entitled September Sunset appeared in the Summer, 2007 edition of Upland Almanac. He is a regular contributor to The Spaniel Journal on a range of gun dog training topics. One of his series of articles, The Dixie Chronicles, was nominated in 2006 for an award from the prestigious Dog Writers' Association of America.

Tony Roettger is a professional gun dog trainer and breeder, whose dogs have won and placed in numerous field trials. He owns and operates Roettger Ridge Kennels in North Branch, Minnesota and regularly contributes to multiple magazines on gun dog training. Tony is the co-author with Chip Schleider of Urban Gun Dogs: Training Flushing Dogs for Home and Field. He is also an avid upland game and waterfowl hunter.

Indoor Drills

"HUP" DRILL

With your dog on a leash in front of you, give the command "hup" as you put his dog bowl full of food down. Push his rear down if he does not "hup." Then give him the "OK" release command. Progress to doing this off lead after a week or two. Get your dog used to "hupping" in front of doorways, before going up or down stairs, or into his crate on your command. Always give the command first, and then push his rear down if he does not obey. Do not get into the habit of repeating commands.

Repetition: Keep lessons—short 1 or 2 repetitions depending upon the drill.

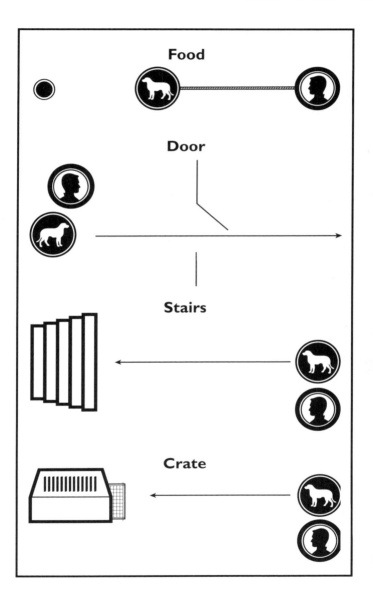

Food

Door

Stairs

Crate

PLACE DRILL

Place a towel on the floor. With your dog on a lead, put your dog on the towel, and give the commands "place" and "hup" in that order. Do not let him off of the towel until you give him the "OK" release command. Continue with this drill for several days. With the dog on lead, but off the towel, give him the "place" command and walk him to the towel. Once he is on the towel give him the "hup" command. Keep him there for a few moments, then release him. When your dog begins to move toward the towel when you give the "place" command, try it off lead. This may take a week or two. Always "hup" him on the towel, then release him. Once he masters the towel. Switch to a dog bed.

Repetition: Repeat 2 or 3 times, and keep lessons short; 10 to 15 minutes.

Step 1

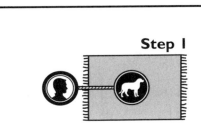

Step 2

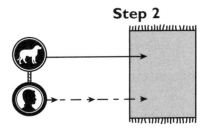

Step 3

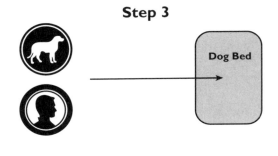

"Here" Drill

On Lead

With your dog on a lead in a blocked (if possible) hallway, "hup" your dog in front of you. Back away from him and, give the "here" command followed by four quick "pips" on the whistle. The dog may come to you on his own. If he does not come immediately, give a quick tug on the lead, but do not reel him in like a fish. When he comes to you, praise him lavishly and immediately release him with the "OK" command.
If you cannot get the dog to stay "hupped" when you back away, have someone restrain the dog lightly then release him when you give the "here" command.

Hint: if you remain low to the ground, in a kneeling position, the puppy is more likely to come bounding into your arms. This little trick will become more useful later.

Repetition: Repeat 2 or 3 times, and keep lessons short; 10 to 15 minutes.

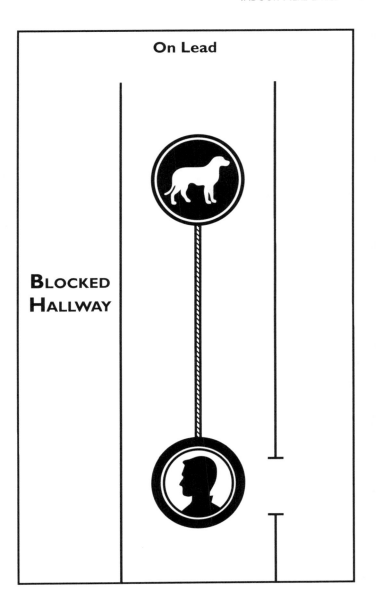

On Lead

BLOCKED HALLWAY

"Here" Drill

Off Lead

With your dog off lead in a blocked (if possible) hallway, "hup" your dog in front of you. Back away from him and, give the "here" command followed by four quick "pips" on the whistle. The dog may come to you on his own. When he comes to you, praise him lavishly and immediately release him with the "OK" command.

As in the previous drill, if you cannot get the dog to stay "hupped" when you back away, have someone restrain the dog lightly then release him when you give the "here" command.

Hint: Do not forget to kneel down or be low to the ground to offer puppy the security and comfort he or she will need.

Repetition: Repeat 2 or 3 times, and keep lessons short; 10 to 15 minutes.

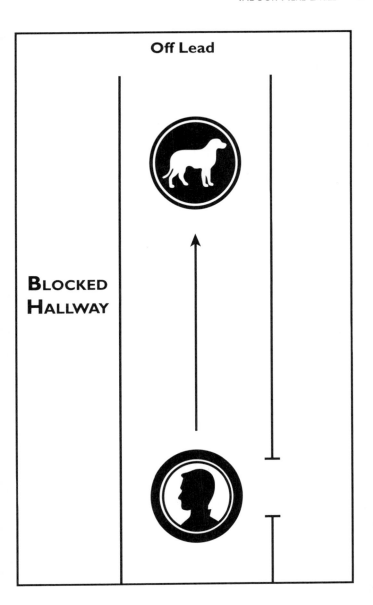

Off Lead

BLOCKED HALLWAY

LEAVE DRILL

With your dog on lead at a normal feeding time, put his dog bowl of food in front of him. When he starts to go for it, give the "leave" command and pull back on the lead. Immediately give the "OK" command and let him eat.

Repetition: Repeat once at dinner time for a week.

Wall Heeling Drill

With your dog on lead in a room or hallway, position your dog close to the wall with a short hold on the lead. Give the "heel" command, and begin walking around the room or hall. If your dog tries to surge ahead, cut him off gently with your knee and say "heel." After several weeks of this, try this off lead again with the dog close to the wall.

Repetition: Keep lessons short; 10 to 15 minutes.

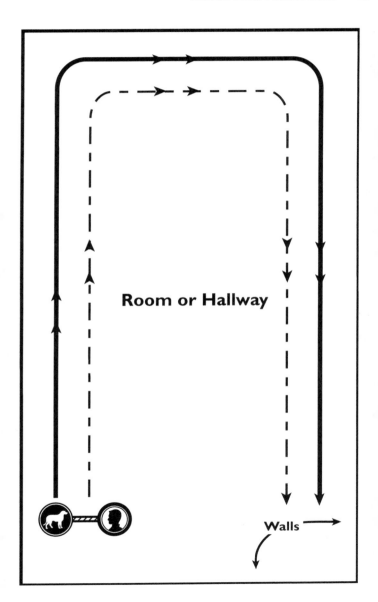

Room or Hallway

Walls →

OPEN AREA HEELING DRILL

After your dog has worked the wall heeling drill for several weeks. Try heeling him with the lead on in an open room, the basement, or the garage. If he starts to surge ahead of you or cut in front of you, go back to the wall heeling drill until you believe he is ready to try the open area drill.

Repetition: Keep lessons short; 10 to 15 minutes.

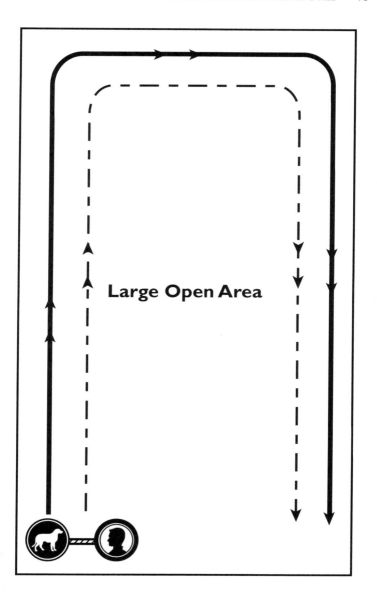

Large Open Area

INITIAL RETRIEVING DRILL

Step 1: Sock Dummy

In blocked (if possible) hallway with your dog off lead, sit down on the floor with a couple of rolled up socks. Tease the dog playfully with the socks and throw them a couple of feet in front of you, the dog should bolt after the socks and pick them up. Kneel down, call "here," and he should come to you. Do not touch or take the socks from the dog's mouth initially, but let him hold them for a moment while you praise him lavishly. After praise, give the "drop" command, gently take the socks from his mouth. Work on making this fun, but do not get into a tug of war contest with the dog. Play within "training" boundaries.

Repetition: Repeat 3 or 4 times.

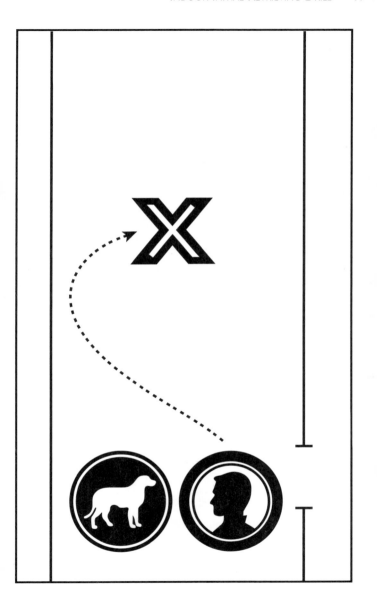

INITIAL RETRIEVING DRILL

Step 2: Small Dummy

After you have worked a while with the basic "here" drill in the hallway, with your dog off lead in a blocked (if possible) hallway, tease the dog playfully with a soft dummy, throw it down the hall, and say the dog's name as the release command. After your sock retrieve work, the dog should bolt after the dummy. Kneel down call "here," and he should come to you. Do not touch or take the dummy from the dog's mouth initially, but let him have for a moment while you praise him lavishly. After praise, give the "drop" command, gently take the dummy from his mouth. Work on the retrieving aspects of the drill, not the delivery.

Repetition: Repeat 3 or 4 times.

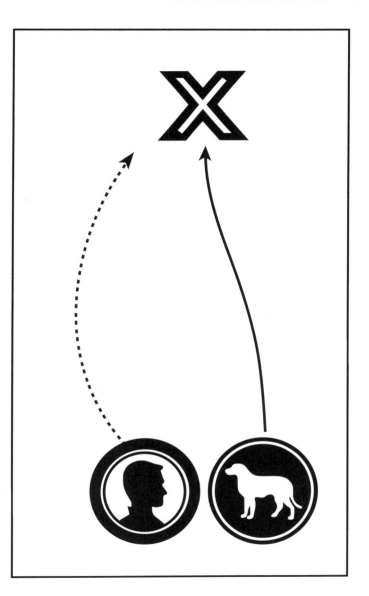

SMALL DUMMY INITIAL RETRIEVING

After you have worked a while with the basic "here" drill in the hallway, move to a large open area such as a garage or basement. As you did in the hallway drill, kneel down call "here," and he should come to you as before. Again, remember not to touch or take the dummy from the dog's mouth initially, but let him have for a moment while you praise him lavishly. After praise, give the "drop" command, gently take the dummy from his mouth. Continue to work on the retrieving aspects of the drill, not the delivery. If he becomes distracted or runs away from you, go back to the hallway drill until you are certain he can make the transition to a larger area.

Hint: Stay low to the ground, kneeling, but do not hover over the pup by leaning over the dog. This will only intimidate the puppy and will potential cause retrieving issues later on. Remember, security and a pat on the head is what the puppy will come to love.

Repetition: Repeat 3 or 4 times.

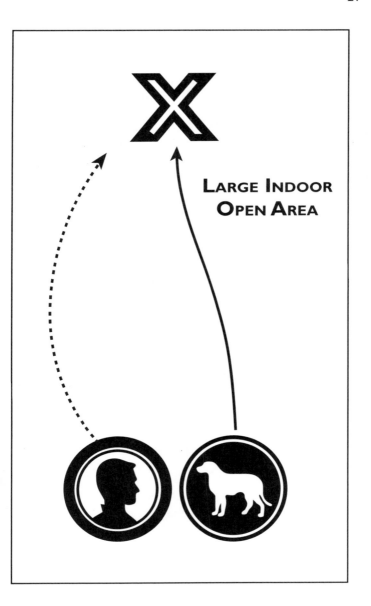

LARGE INDOOR OPEN AREA

PRE-GUNFIRE CONDITIONING DRILL

While your dog is eating dinner, move into the next room, but still within earshot of your dog. Clap your hands loudly once. Over a few days he will grow used to that sound. Gradually close the distance to where you are within a few feet. When he is conditioned to this, begin clapping your hand on the bottom of the bowl a few times lightly but enough to offer a noise that could be considered annoying by fellow family members. Then, give food to puppy. After a few days of this action, alter your feeding time so the puppy is not waiting for you by his bowl. While pup is off playing, clap your hand on the bottom of the bowl. Your dog will begin coming to the noise.
Once he is well conditioned to this, take two blocks of wood and move back into the next room. Again, just after the dog starts to eat, clap the blocks together. Try to not make the sound too loud initially. Over the next week or two narrow the gap consistent with your dog's ability to tolerate the noise. You do not want him to flinch at all. If he becomes the least bit sensitive to the sound, cease and go back to the hand clap.

Repetition: Repeat once at dinner time for a week.

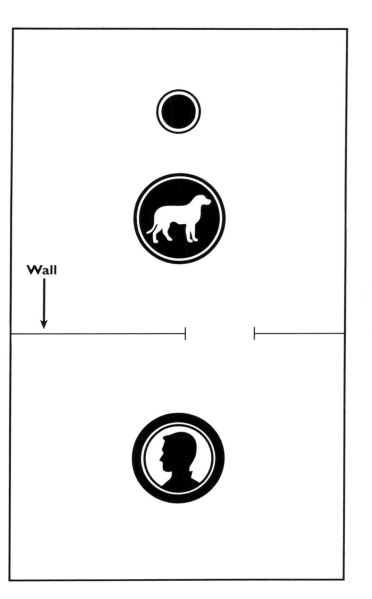

Wall

INTRODUCTION TO TAKING A LINE DRILL

Place a dummy at one end of the blocked hallway while your dog is watching. Move with your dog to the end of the hallway. With your dog off lead and "hupped" to your side, indicate a line with the knife edge of your hand toward the dummy in front of the dog's nose, but not blocking the dog's view. Give your dog his name as the release command. He should easily make the retrieve. The objective is to have your dog associate the line of your hand with the presence of a dummy or bird for a retrieve down field.

Repetition: Repeat 4 or 5 times.

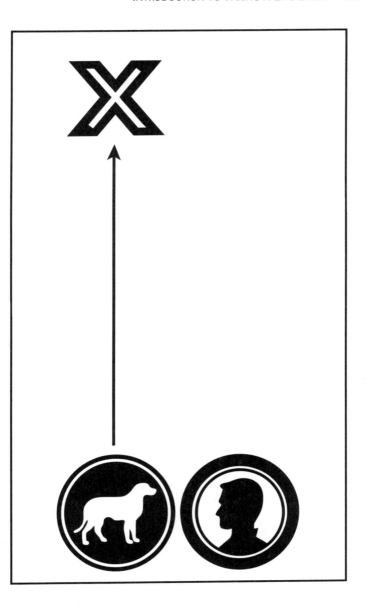

Pre-Steadying Drill

In your hallway or large open area, "hup" the dog several feet in front of you. Toss a soft dummy behind you at the same time you blow a single "pip" on the whistle. If your dog remains "hupped" release the dog for the retrieve. If he breaks, block him from making the retrieve with your body. Relocate him back to his original position. Pick up the dummy and try again. Do not let him make the retrieve if he breaks. Once he has mastered this drill move to throwing the dummy to the left or right. Always try to throw the dummy in such a way as to prevent him from making the retrieve should he break.

Repetition: Repeat 3 or 4 times.

Thrown Behind

Thrown to the Left

Thrown to the Right

Outdoor Drills

Advanced "Hup" Drill

With your dog on a 30-foot checkcord, give the dog the "hup" command followed by one "pip" on the whistle. Back slowly away from him while looking at him. If he breaks, and he surely will the first couple of times, say "no" or "aaah" and place him back where he was. The checkcord enables you to control him, and keeps him from running and playing. Once he "hups" and remains "hupped" while you are about 5 feet away, return to the dog. Do not call him to you, as this often will encourage him to give into his natural tendency to run to you. Return to the dog, give him the release command, and praise him.

Repetition: 4 or 5 times.

Step 1

Step 2

5-10 feet

Step 3

OUTDOOR PLACE DRILL

As you did inside, place a towel on the ground in your yard. With your dog on a lead, but off the towel, give him the "place" command and walk him to the towel. Once he is on the towel give him the "hup" command. Keep him there for a few moments, then release him. When your dog begins to move toward the towel when you give the "place" command followed by a single "pip" on the whistle, try it next with a 30 foot checkcord in place of the lead, then without lead. This may take a week or two. Always "hup" him on the towel, then release him. The outdoor environment often adds distractions that sometimes makes a dog regress.

Repetition: Repeat 2 or 3 times, and keep lessons short; 10 to 15 minutes.

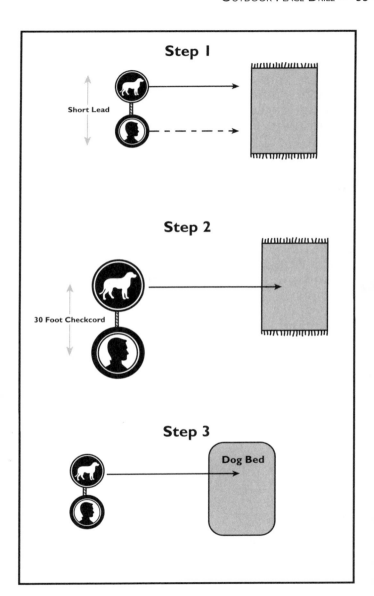

OUTDOOR BASIC "HERE" DRILL

With your dog on a 30-foot checkcord, let the dog wander in front of you, play, or do his personal business. When you feel like the dog will respond to you, give the "here" command followed by four quick "pips" on the whistle. The dog should, if you have practiced this indoors, come to you. If he does not come immediately, give a quick tug on the checkcord, but do not reel him in like a fish. When he comes to you, praise him lavishly and immediately release him with the "OK" command to play or wander.

Hint: Remember to kneel and stay low on the ground and your dog will more than likely come into you.

Repetition: Repeat 2 or 3 times, and keep lessons short; 10 to 15 minutes.

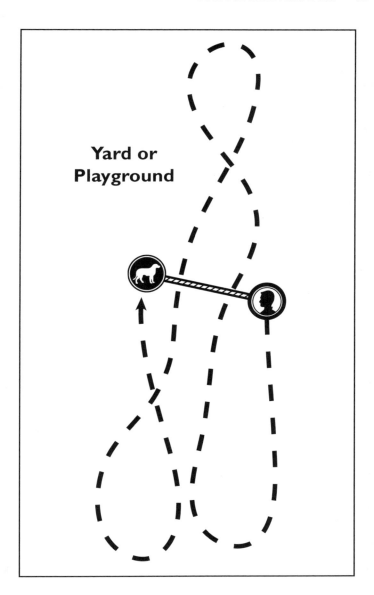

Yard or Playground

BASIC OFF LEAD "HERE" DRILL

With your dog off lead and no checkcord, position the dog about 5 to 10 feet from you and "hup" him. Back slowly away, and do not take your eyes off the dog. Give "here" command followed by four quick "pips" on the whistle. The dog should, if you have practiced this outdoors on a checkcord, come to you. When he comes to you, praise him lavishly. If he does not, run him down, and go back to using the checkcord until you are ready to try it again. Gradually lengthen the distances.

Hint: If your dog is having problems, kneel, stay low, do not hover.

Repetition: Repeat 2 or 3 times, and keep lessons short; 10 to 15 minutes.

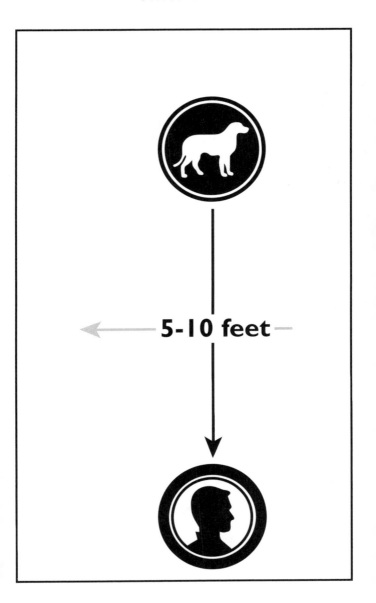

5-10 feet

ADVANCED "HERE" DRILL

With your dog off lead, let the dog wander in front of you, play, or do his personal business. When you feel like the dog will respond to you, give the "here" command followed by four quick "pips" on the whistle. The dog should come to you. When he comes to you, praise him lavishly and immediately release him with the "OK" command to play or wander. If he does not come when you call. Run him down, and go back a step to the previous drill.

Hint: As before, if your dog is having problems, kneel and stay low.

Repetition: Repeat 2 or 3 times, and keep lessons short; 10 to 15 minutes.

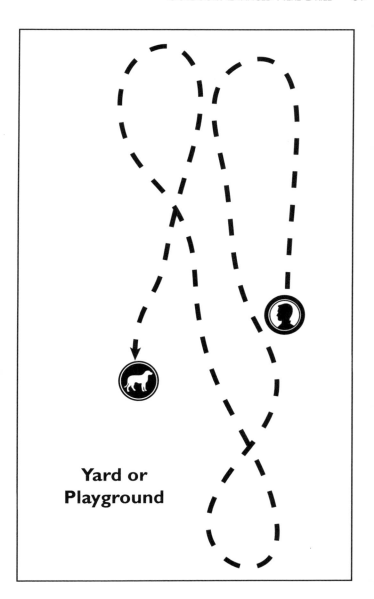

Yard or Playground

Outdoor "Leave" Drill

With your dog on a checkcord, throw a dummy, toss a bird, or spray some scent (duck or pheasant scent is commercially available). Let your dog wander toward the area (do not release for the retrieve by calling the dog's name). Once the dog is in the vicinity of the dummy, bird, or scent, but before he has it in his mouth, give the "leave" command, and tug, but do not pull, the dog back toward you. Quickly give the command "here" as you bring your dog back to you. Only attempt this training when you feel like it will not affect the dog's retrieving desire.

Repetition: Repeat 3 or 4 times.

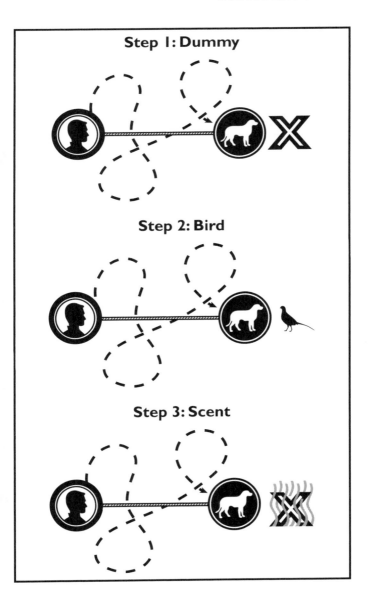

Outdoor Wall Heeling Drill

With your dog on lead along an exterior wall or fence, position your dog close to the wall with a short hold on the lead as you did for the indoor drill. Give the "heel" command, and begin walking around the wall or fence. If your dog tries to surge ahead, again cut him off gently with your knee and say "heel." After several weeks of this, try this off lead again with the dog close to the fence.

Repetition: Keep lessons short; 10 to 15 minutes.

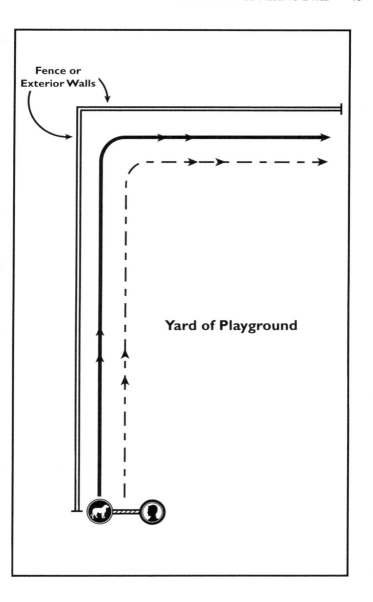

Fence or Exterior Walls

Yard of Playground

Outdoor Heeling Drill

Move to this drill only after your dog has mastered the outdoor wall drill. With your dog on a short lead. Give the "heel" command, and begin walking on the driveway or sidewalk. If your dog tries to surge ahead or cross in front of your legs, say "no" sharply, then say "heel" again, and reposition him at your side with a sharp yank on the lead. Some dogs will make the transition from the wall drill more easily to pavement than others. Take a step back to the wall or fence if he does not appear to be making progress. Move to off lead, only when you are extremely confident in his abilities.

Repetition: Keep lessons short; 10 to 15 minutes.

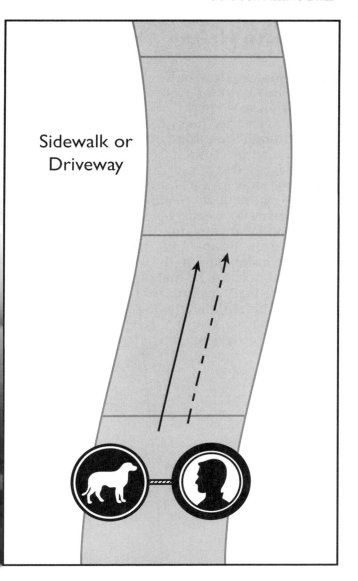

Sidewalk or
Driveway

ADVANCED HEELING "HUP" DRILL

Move to this drill only after your dog has mastered the outdoor wall drill and your dog heels well on a sidewalk. With your dog on a short lead, give the "heel" command, and begin walking through the yard or field. If your dog tries to surge ahead or cross in front of your legs, say "no" sharply, then say "heel" again, and reposition him at your side with a sharp yank on the lead. Dogs often have a more difficult time heeling in fields owing to smells and other distractions. Periodically, have your dog "hup." While he his "hupped," walk around him, but do not let him move. Take a step back to the fence or sidewalk if he does not appear to be making progress. Again, move to off lead heeling, only when you are confident of his abilities.

Repetition: Keep lessons short; 10 to 15 minutes.

Yard,
Playground,
or Field

BASIC QUARTERING DRILL

In a playground area, face the wind with your dog on a 30-foot checkcord "hupped" in front of you. Give your dog the "get out" or "hunt'em up" command and let him begin to quarter. Ideally, he should be about 10 yards in front of you. Let him hunt naturally about 10 yards to your left or right. To turn him give him two short "pips" on the whistle and then a quick tug. Do not haul with the rope. Continue about 40 yards downfield, stop him, recall him, then heel him back to the starting point.

Repetition: 2 or 3 times.

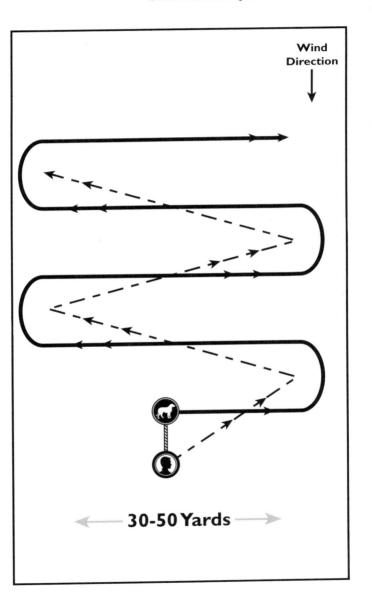

Wind Direction

← 30-50 Yards →

ADVANCED QUARTERING DRILL

With the wind in your face and your dog off lead "hup" him in front of you. Give your dog the "get out" or "hunt'em up" command and let him begin to quarter. Let him hunt naturally about 10 yards to your left or right. To turn him give him two short "pips" on the whistle. Continue about 40 yards downfield, stop him, recall him, then heel him back to the start point.

Repetition: 2 or 3 times.

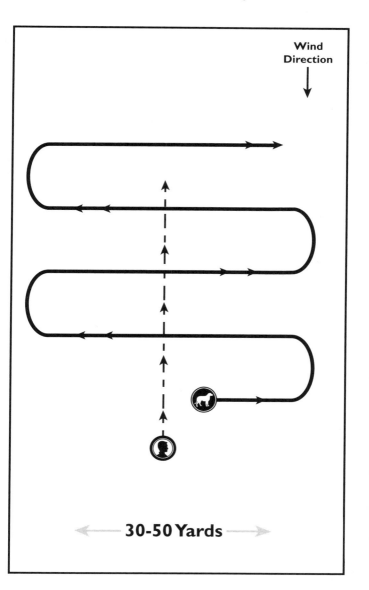

Wind Direction

30-50 Yards

Advanced Quartering "Hup" Drill

With the wind in your face and your dog off lead "hup" him in front of you. Give your dog the "get out" or "hunt'em up" command and let him begin to quarter. Let him hunt naturally about 10 yards to your left or right. To turn him give him two short "pips" on the whistle. Periodically, but not at every turn, give him a "pip" on the whistle to "hup" him. Hold in this position for a few moments, then give him the "get out" command. Continue about 40 yards downfield, stop him, recall him, then heel him back to the start point.

Repetition: 2 or 3 times.

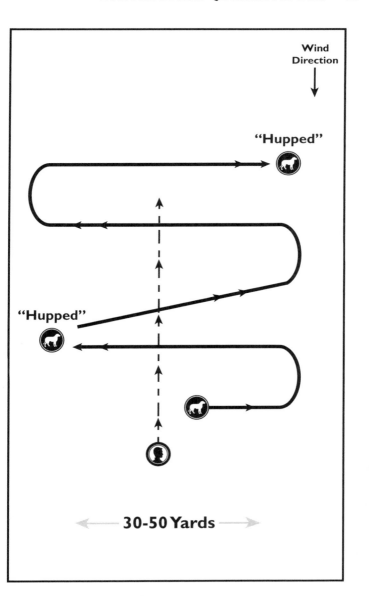

ADVANCED DOWNWIND QUARTERING

With the wind at your back, and your dog off lead "hup" him in front of you. Give your dog the "get out"or "hunt'em up" command and let him begin to quarter. He will naturally quarter quite differently with the wind at your back. His patterns will be more down the field and back to you. To turn him give him two short "pips" on the whistle, but try not to over control him in this exercise. Continue about 40 yards downfield, stop him, recall him, then heel him back to the start point.

Note: Dogs vary in their downwind patterns. The best patterns may look more like figure 8's.

Repetition: 2 or 3 times.

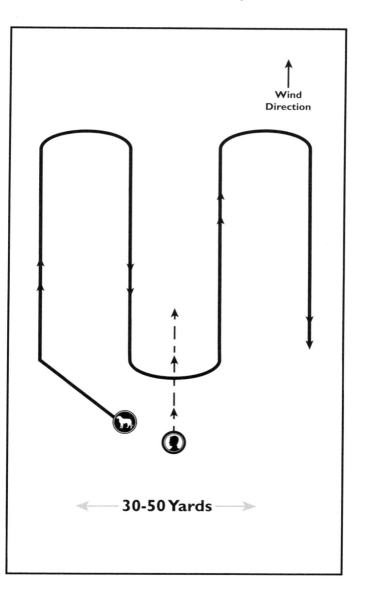

Wind
Direction

← 30-50 Yards →

Quartering Steadying Drill

Undertake this drill when your dog is very line steady and proficient at quartering. Hide a bumper in your coat so the dog does not know you have it. With the wind in your face and your dog off lead "hup" him in front of you. Give your dog the "get out" or "hunt'em up" command to begin quartering. Let him make a couple of turns on your course. As he rounds a corner, toss the bumper and give him one "pip" on the whistle. He should "hup" readily. Give the release command to make the retrieve. Continue about 40 yards downfield, stop him, recall him, then heel him back to the start point.

Repetition: 2 or 3 times.

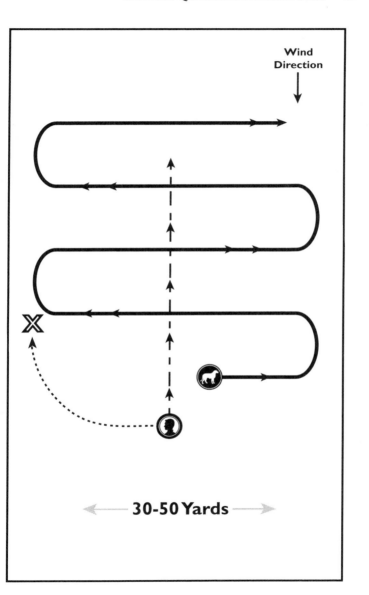

Wind
Direction

X

30-50 Yards

ADVANCED BRACE QUARTERING DRILL

This drill should be undertaken in conjunction with a friend and his dog and only when your dog is extremely proficient on handling quartering and "hups" readily to whistle commands. Lay out a course with center flags or cones about 100 yards in length and about 75 yards wide. With the wind in your face, start the dogs quartering downfield, but try to keep them from crossing the center line. Both dogs proceed down their individual courses. Periodically, one handler "hups" his dog while the other makes a retrieve of a thrown bumper thus "honoring" the retrieve.

Repetition: 1 or 2 runs of the course.

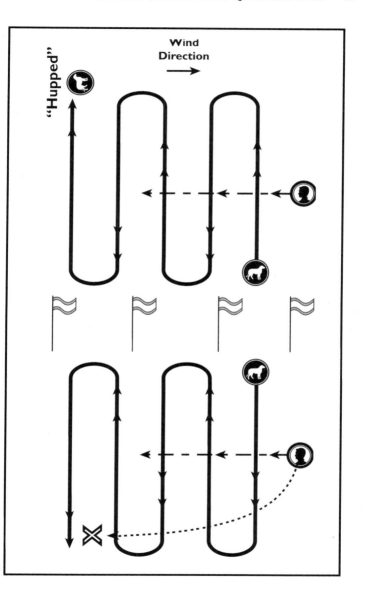

OUTDOOR GUNFIRE
PRE-CONDITIONING

With dog "hupped" next to you, toss a dummy about 20-30 yards in front of the dog. With the dummy still in the air, clap your hands loudly as you did during the pre-gunfire conditioning drill indoors. Make sure he remains steady and does not flinch in any way. Give your dog his name as a release command and let go of the lead. He should run to the dummy and pick it up. Give him four "pips" on the whistle to recall him. As your dog gains confidence introduce the wooden blocks to simulate gunfire.

Repetition: 3 or 4 times. Do not over do this; stop if he shows any signs of flinching.

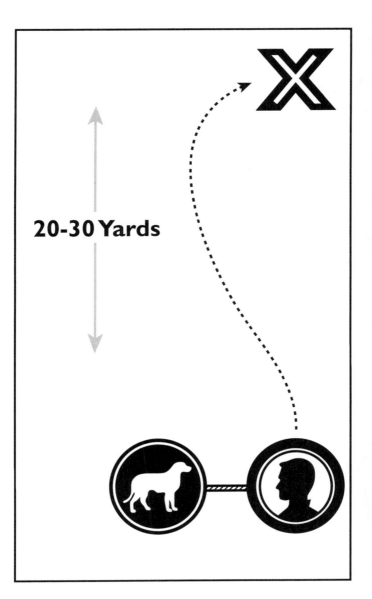

20-30 Yards

ADVANCED GUNFIRE CONDITIONING

Only after you are certain that your dog will not flinch, and after extensive conditioning with the wooden blocks, quarter your dog in an open field. Toss a dead bird or bumper as far in front of your dog as you can while simultaneously firing a starter or primer pistol behind your back while the bird is up in the air. Allow him to make the retrieve. Only after your dog demonstrates no reaction whatsoever to the pistol, progress to a shotgun with a light popper load. When introducing a dog to gunfire in this manner it helps to have live birds to further reduce the impact of the noise. As in all cases if your dog demonstrates the slightest sensitivity to the gun shot, cease immediately, and revert to the pre-gun fire conditioning drills.

Repetition: 2 or 3 times.

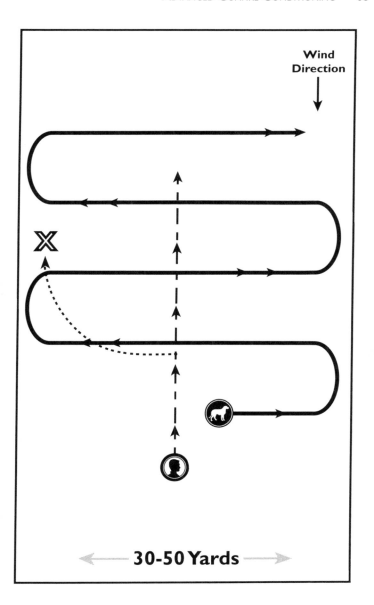

Wind Direction

X

30-50 Yards

SINGLE MARKED RETRIEVES

With your dog "hupped" next to you, restrain him with the lead, but do not attach it to the collar or slip it over his head if your are using a slip lead. Instead, merely wrap the lead around the dog's neck such that if you drop one end, the dog will be free. Grasp both ends, toss a dummy about 20-30 yards in front of the dog and give one "pip" on the whistle. Give your dog his name as a release command and let go of the lead. He should run to the dummy and pick it up. Give him four "pips" on the whistle to recall him.

Repetition: 4 or 5 times. Do not over do this; leave the drill with the dog always wanting one more retrieve.

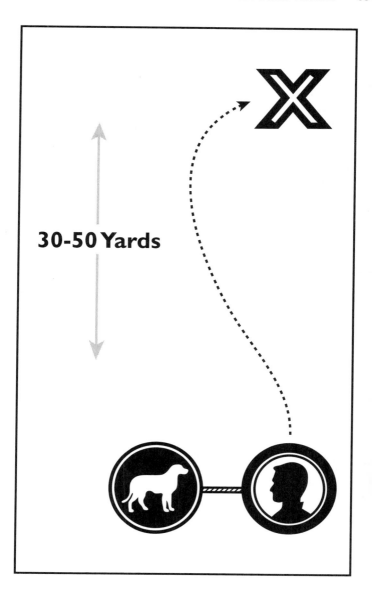

30-50 Yards

INTRODUCTION TO WATER RETRIEVES

After the dog is retrieving dummies on land well and only after the water is warm, you can begin initial water retrieves. Locate a pond with a shallow area in which you know the dog will be able to stand up without swimming. With the dog off lead at your side, tease the dog with the dummy, and throw it in the water a couple of feet in front of the dog where he will have to go into the water to make the retrieve, but will not have to swim. He should make the retrieve, but if he does not enter the water on his own, do not throw him in the water. Pick up the dummy and move it closer, continue to work on this until he succeeds. Gradually lengthen throws to 5 yards as the dog builds confidence.

Repetition: 2 or 3 retrieves. Always leave the drill with the dog wanting one more retrieve.

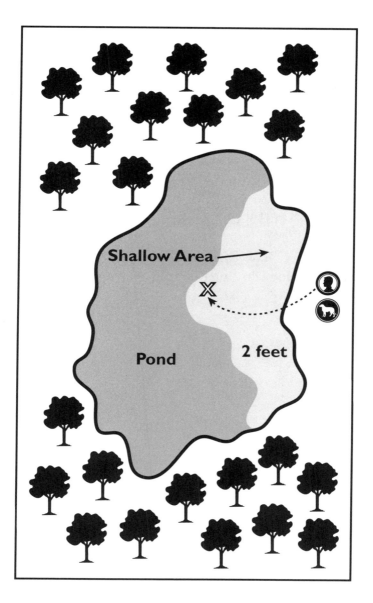

Shallow Area

X

Pond

2 feet

SINGLE MARKED WATER RETRIEVES

After the dog is retrieving dummies that are thrown several feet from the bank and is swimming to them, throw a dummy no more than 5 yards from the bank (put a string on the dummy should the dog refuse the retrieve in order to retrieve the dummy without taking a swim). At this point he should be able to make the retrieve. If he does not, pull the dummy in a little at a time until the dog makes the retrieve. As the dog builds confidence, you may lengthen the retrieves to 20 yards or more.

Repetition: 2 or 3 retrieves. Always leave the drill with the dog wanting one more retrieve.

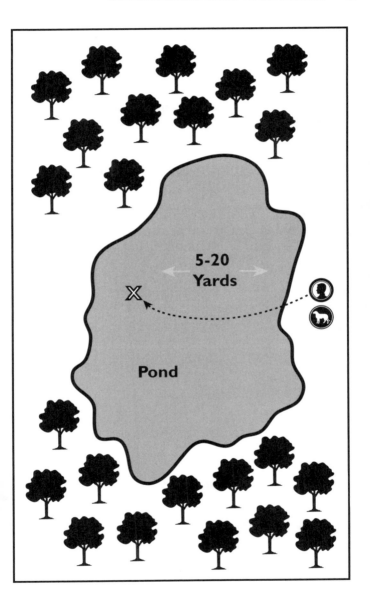

LINE STEADYING DRILL

As you did indoors, "hup" the dog several feet in front of you. Toss a soft dummy behind you at the same time you blow a single "pip" on the whistle. If your dog remains "hupped" release the dog for the retrieve. If he breaks, block him from making the retrieve with your body. Relocate him back to his original position. Pick up the dummy and try again. Do not let him make the retrieve if he breaks. Once he has mastered this drill move to throwing the dummy to the left or right. Always try to throw the dummy in such a way as to prevent him from making the retrieve should he break.

Repetition: Repeat 3 or 4 times.

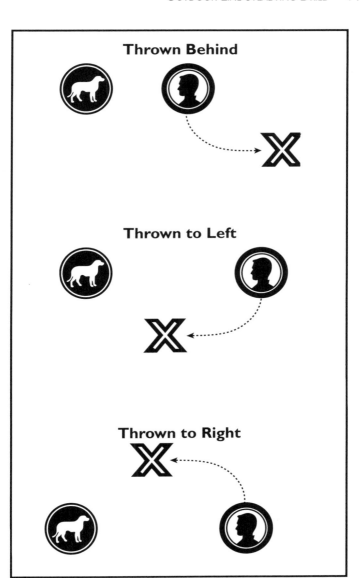

SINGLE MARKED STEADY RETRIEVES

After your dog is line steady and with dog "hupped" next to you off lead, toss a dummy about 20-30 yards in front of the dog and give one "pip" on the whistle. If he breaks, block him to keep him from making the retrieve. If he is steady, give your dog his name as a release command and let go of the lead. He should run to the dummy and pick it up. Give him four "pips" on the whistle to recall him.

Repetition: 4 or 5 times. Do not over do this; leave the drill with the dog wanting one more retrieve.

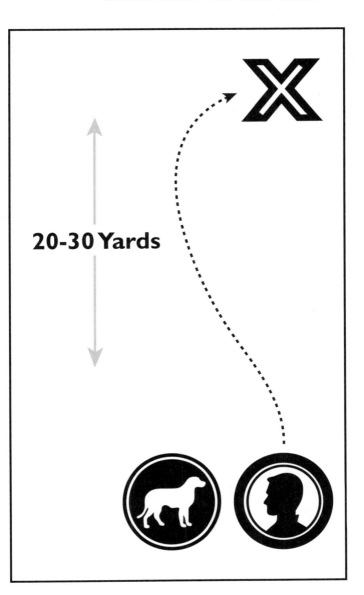

BASEBALL DIAMOND DRILL

Here the dog must be perfectly line steady, "Hup" him in the middle of a field off lead (pitcher's mound). Back up approximately 10 yards with 3 bumpers (home plate). Toss one to your left (3rd base) , then one to right (1st base), then one over the dog's head (2nd base). Raise your arm straight up and give him the "back" command. He should go for the last bumper you threw behind him. Once he makes the retrieve, reposition him on the pitcher's mound, extend your right arm and give the "over" command. He should pick up the 1st base bumper. Again reposition him on the pitcher's mound, and extend your left arm. He should pick up the 3rd base bumper. If the dog breaks on any throw go back to line steadying drills.

Repetition: Repeat 3 or 4 times.

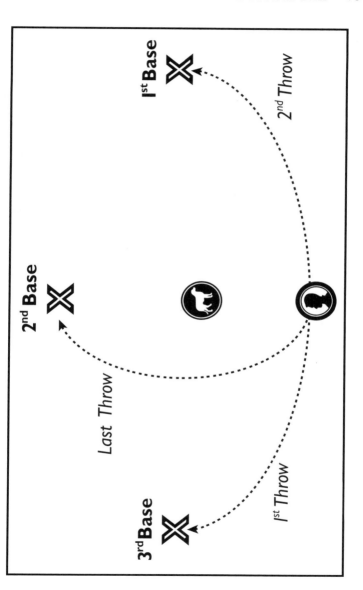

BEGINNING DUMMY LAUNCH DRILL

Dummy launcher drills should be undertaken only when the dog is extremely line steady, very conditioned to gunfire, and in an area that allows shooting. Choose your location carefully. With the dog "hupped" at your side, slide the dummy on the launcher, break the launcher open, and load the launcher with a "green" (or light) load. Make sure that the launcher is pointed away from the dog and other people when you close the breach. Point the launcher down range and up in the air to ensure that the dummy does not travel too far on the first shot. Wear a heavy glove to protect your hand as well as hearing protection, and protective glasses. Fire the launcher, and give the dog the release command. Use "yellow" (or medium) loads once your dog is retrieving well at shorter distances.

Repetition: 2 or 3 times.

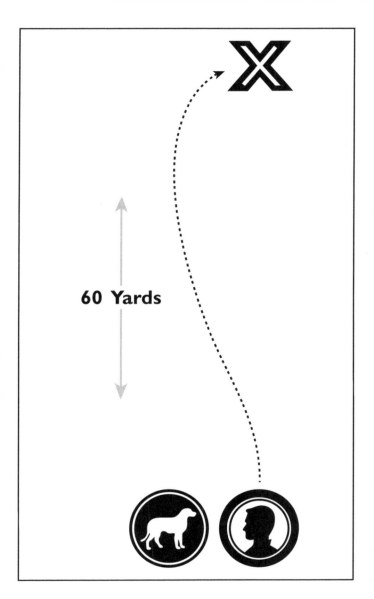

60 Yards

DOUBLE MARKED RETRIEVES

After the dog is consistently retrieving single marked retrieves well and is line steady, move to doubles. "Hup" him next to you and throw the first dummy with a single "pip" on the whistle (called the "memory" bird, he should not break. Throw next dummy (called the "diversion" dummy or bird) again with one "pip" on the whistle. Send him to the diversion dummy first. When he makes the retrieve line him up for the memory dummy and release him.

Repetition: 4 or 5 retrieves. Always leave the drill with the dog wanting one more retrieve.

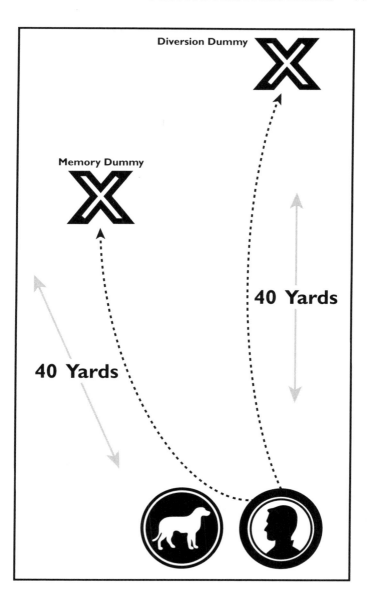

Diversion Dummy

Memory Dummy

40 Yards

40 Yards

DOUBLE MARKED WATER RETRIEVES

Move to doubles after the dog is consistently retrieving single marked water retrieves well and is line steady. "Hup" him next to you and throw the memory dummy into the water with a single "pip" on the whistle. Again, he should not break. Then throw diversion dummy in the water again with one "pip" on the whistle. Send him to the diversion dummy first. When he makes the retrieve line him up for the memory dummy and release him.

Repetition: 2 or 3 retrieves. Always leave the drill with the dog wanting one more retrieve.

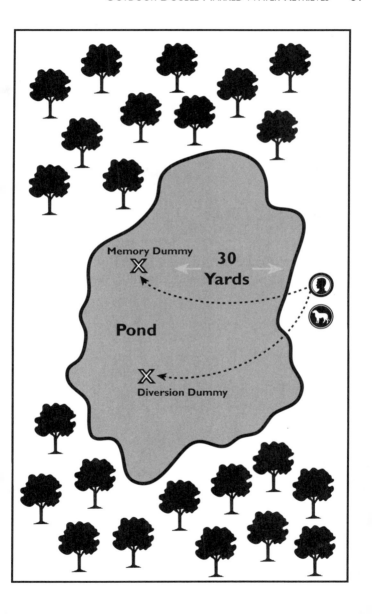

BASIC LINING DRILL

With your dog on lead, take a flag on a stick or cone and place it in the ground, and put a dummy next to it making certain your dog sees the dummy placed. Walk your dog about 15 yards away, "hup" him, and take the lead off. Give him a line to the flag and release him. He should go readily to the flag and retrieve the dummy. As he gains proficiency with this, place 2 dummies on the ground so he can see them. He should make these retrieves easily. After a week of this drill, place the dummies next to the flag in advance so he does not see. He should by now associate the flag with a dummy. Continue with the drill with 3 dummies. Increase the distance as the dog handles the retrieves.

Repetition: 3 or 4 times.

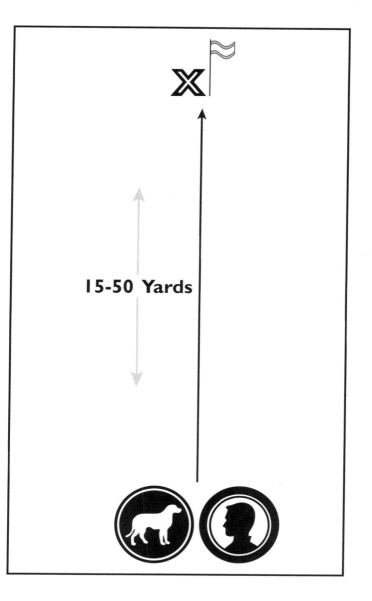

15-50 Yards

ADVANCED LINING DRILL

This drill builds heavily upon the previous drill. Set up a course with three flags or cones. Place 2 dummies at each flag. Line up your dog with flag No. 1 and give him the release command. When he returns with the dummy line him to flag No. 2, then flag No. 3. Start over at flag No. 1 for the second dummy. When he is retrieving well at 30 yards move the flags out to 50 yards each. Concentrate on this drill series for a couple of weeks before moving to the blind retrieves.

Repetition: 2 or 3 times.

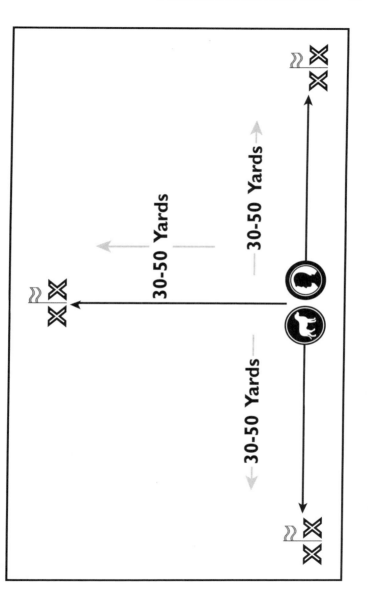

DOUBLE DUMMY LAUNCH DRILL

Once you are comfortable with singles using the green (light) loads, and your dog retrieves short doubles well, progress to doubles. Again with the dog "hupped" at your side, slide the dummy on the launcher, break the launcher open, and load the launcher with a green load. Make sure that the launcher is pointed away from the dog and other people when you close the breach. Point the launcher down range and up in the air to ensure that the dummy does not travel too far on the first shot. Reload and repeat. Make sure that you wear a heavy glove to protect your hand and wear hearing protection, when you fire the launcher. Give the dog the release command. Move to "yellow" (medium) and "red" (heavy) loads as your dog gains confidence.

Repetition: 2 or 3 times.

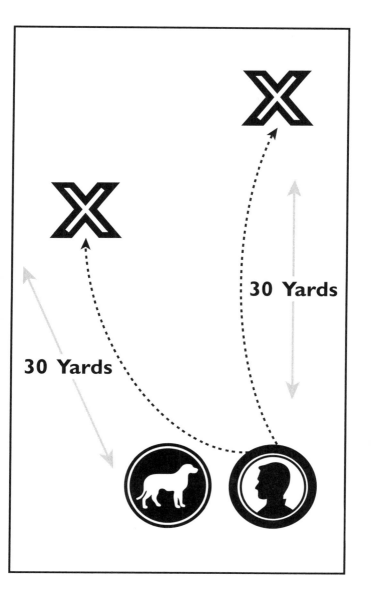

30 Yards

30 Yards

TRIPLE DUMMY LAUNCH DRILL

Once you are comfortable with singles and doubles using the "yellow" loads, try triples. Again with the dog "hupped" at your side, slide the dummy on the launcher, break the launcher open, and load the launcher with a "green" load. Make sure that the launcher is pointed away from the dog and other people when you close the breach. Point the launcher down range and up in the air to ensure that the dummy does not travel too far on the first shot. Reload and repeat twice more. Make sure that you wear a heavy glove to protect your hand and hearing protection, when you fire the launcher. Give the dog the release command. Again, move to "yellow" loads as your dog gains confidence.

Repetition: 2 or 3 times.

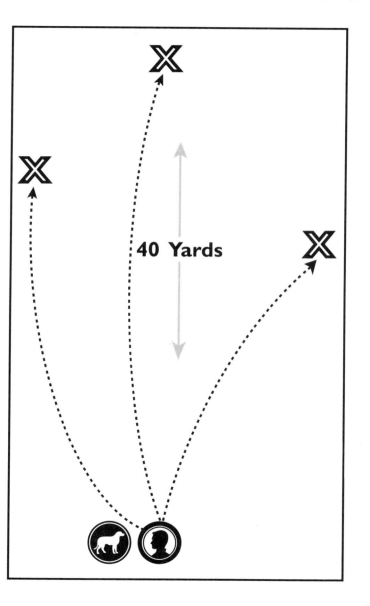

40 Yards

TRIPLE MARKED WATER RETRIEVES

Move to triples after the dog is consistently retrieving double marked water retrieves well and remains line steady. "Hup" him next to you and throw the first memory dummy into the water with a single "pip" on the whistle. Again, he should not break. Throw a second memory dummy with one "pip" on the whistle. Then throw the diversion bird again with "pip." Send him to the diversion dummy first. When he makes the retrieve line him up for the memory dummy (the second one you threw) and release him. Finally, send him to the first memory dummy.

Repetition: 1 or 2 repetitions. Always leave the drill with the dog wanting one more retrieve.

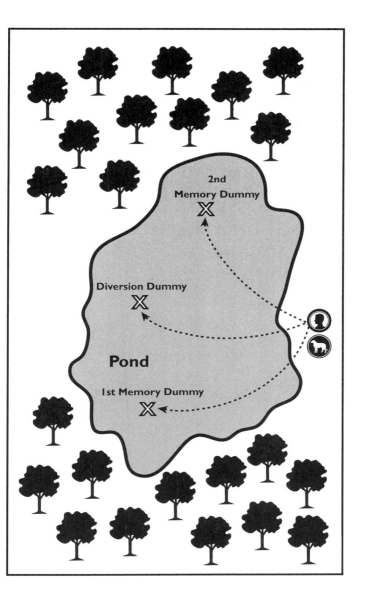

Basic Hunt Dead Drill

While practicing heeling your dog in the yard, park, field or playground, drop a dummy so that your dog does not see it or the fall. Continue to heel the dog about 10 yards further. Stop, take your dog off lead, and give him a line to the dummy. Use his name as a release command and also the command "dead bird." If you have done your line drills, he should have no trouble. He may still hunt or quarter slightly.

Repetition: 1 or 2 times in the course of your heeling drill.

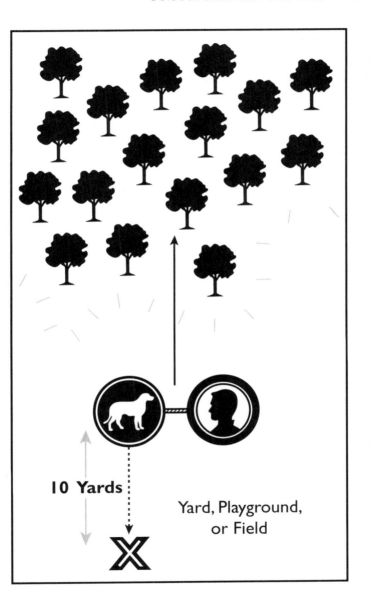

10 Yards

Yard, Playground,
or Field

INTERMEDIATE BLIND RETRIEVES

As your dog gains confidence with the heel and drop hunt dead, progress to longer land blinds. Preposition a dummy in a park without your dog seeing it. Again, give him a line to dummy and Start with a 20 yard blind, and progress to longer 40 and 50 yard blinds.

Repetition: Keep lessons short; 10 to 15 minutes.

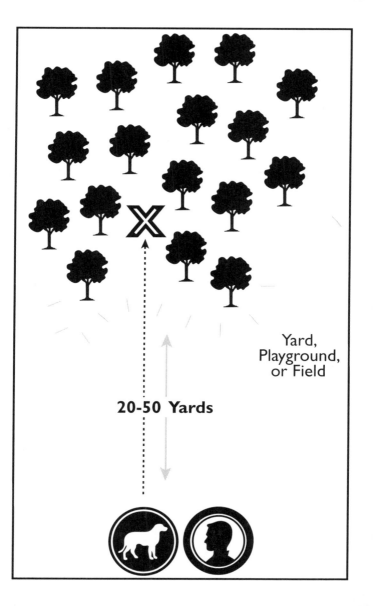

ADVANCED BLIND RETRIEVES

This drill should be undertaken only when your dog is extremely proficient on handling (overs, backs, and "hup" to whistle), can take a line for at least 50 to 60 yards, and has gained proficiency with simple blind retrieves in light cover. Begin to introduce hazards that the dog must cross in order to be able to accomplish the blind retrieve. Start simple and increase both the distances and the hazards as your dog gains confidence. Do not rush this. Blind retrieves take much practice as well as thought in laying them out.

Repetition:1 or 2 retrieves depending upon distance.

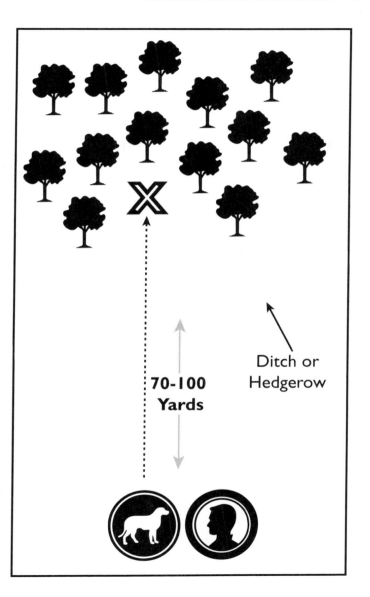

Ditch or
Hedgerow

70-100
Yards

INTRODUCTION TO BLIND WATER RETRIEVES

Once your dog is taking a line, performing well on land blinds, understands that the flag always indicates that a dummy is there, and can swim very well, he is prepared to start training for water blinds. Find a pond close to your home that has a narrow strip of water, no more than 10 yards wide, separating two banks. With your dog on a lead and at heel, place the flag on one side of the pond and drop a dummy. Heel your dog over to the other side bank, "hup" him next to you, and slip off the lead. Give him a line to the flag and release him. After your practice sessions on land, he should associate the flag with the dummy and make the retrieve. Try to keep him from running the bank back to you, by moving to the right or left, depending upon the pond, to make him swim to you.

Repetition: 4 or 5 retrieves.

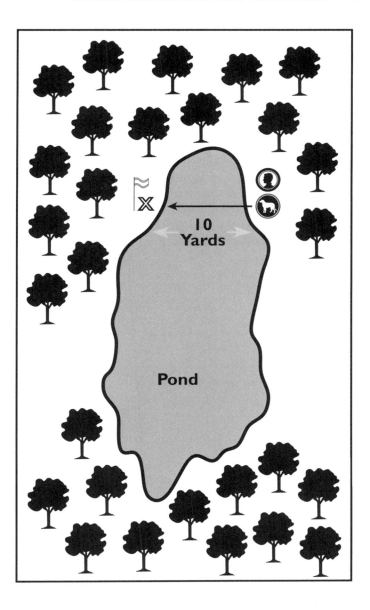

INTERMEDIATE BLIND WATER RETRIEVES

Increase the distance of your flag drills once your dog has thoroughly mastered the short 10 yard course. Ensure that you have taught him basic handling drills such as overs and backs before making the jump to a 40 yard unmarked (but with location indicated by the flag) retrieve across the pond. Keep the sessions short and the repetitions down.

Repetition: 2 or 3 retrieves.

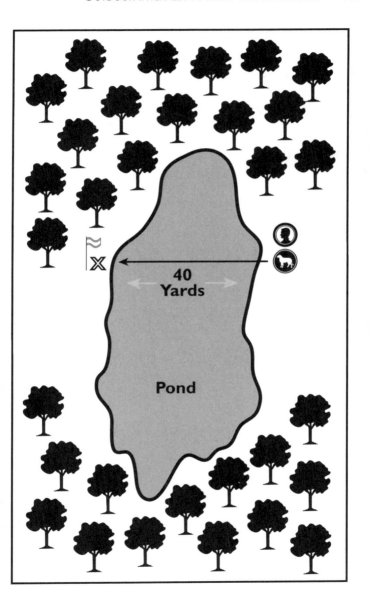

ADVANCED BLIND WATER RETRIEVES

Remove the flag once your dog has thoroughly mastered the short 40 yard course. Continue to re-enforce the basic handling drills such as overs and backs to ensure that the dog will master the 40 yard unmarked retrieve across the pond. Keep the sessions short and the repetitions down.

Repetition: 2 or 3 retrieves.

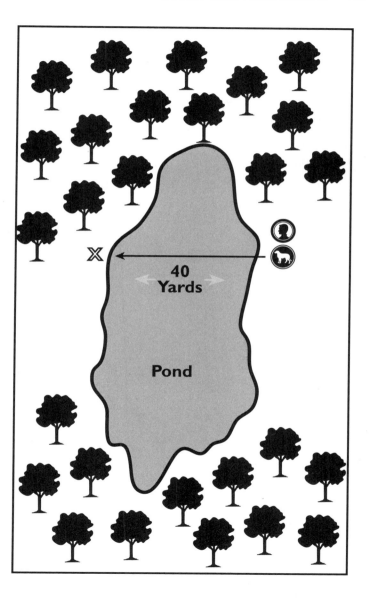

40
Yards

Pond

VERY ADVANCED BLIND WATER RETRIEVES

As your dog gains confidence in you and his ability to make blinds. Increase the distance of the water blind and the complexity. These are limited solely by your imagination and the facilities you have at your disposal. As in all drills, if it is too difficult, drop back a level, and increase the degree of difficulty for the dog only when he is truly ready for the next level.

Repetition: 1 or 2 retrieves.

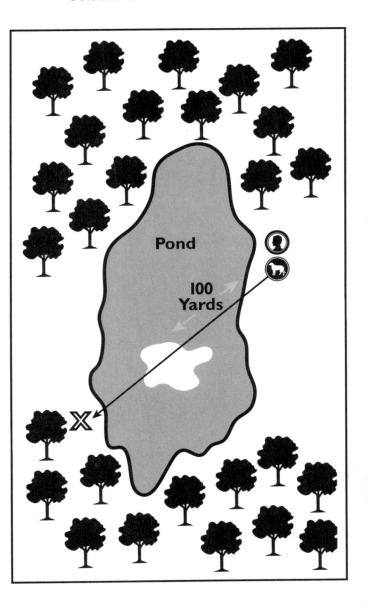

Notes

NOTES

_____

_____

_____

_____

_____

_____

_____

_____

_____

_____

_____

_____

_____

_____

_____

_____

_____

_____

Notes

NOTES

_____

_____

_____

_____

_____

_____

_____

_____

_____

_____

_____

_____

_____

_____

_____

_____

Notes

NOTES

_____

_____

_____

_____

_____

_____

_____

_____

_____

_____

_____

_____

_____

_____

_____

_____

_____

_____